simple

WHOLE 4 MEALS

whole foods, 4 ingredients,
plus a touch of spice

By

Pam Terrell

Integrative Health Practitioner,
Certified Hallelujah Acres Health Minister
& Certified Live Food Chef

Terrell, Pam

Whole 4 Meals / by Pam Terrell

Team Terrell Publishing

www.PamelaTerrell.com

Medical Warning and Disclaimer

The information in this book is not intended as medical advice or to replace a one-on-one relationship with a qualified health care professional. It is intended as a sharing of knowledge and information from the research and experience of Pam Terrell. We encourage you to make your own health care decisions based upon your research and in partnership with a qualified health care professional.

ISBN-13: 978-0-9980187-3-7

This cookbook is dedicated to:

My taste-tester husband, Jeff. It was fun seeing him
enjoy this process as he sampled his way through
the recipes and helped me choose photos.
His support is priceless and one of my biggest blessings.

My son, Alex, who is always super supportive of my creative projects.

My mother, Sandy, who is probably my #1 fan in the kitchen.

Table of Contents

Section I:

Healthy Whole Food

Playing with Food

I love colorful, vibrant, and healthy plant foods! I also like to play and have fun, don't you? I guess, technically, cooking is "playing with food", so it makes sense the kitchen is my happy place!

It wasn't always this way. It took 20 years of intense health challenges to lead me to the healthiest diet and lifestyle for me, finally allowing my body to heal. ** Although painful, those experiences were blessings in disguise. Each taught me about myself, my purpose, what divine love is, and most importantly about gratitude.

I became flexible and super creative in the kitchen, especially with a limited ingredient list. It is interesting how my brain likes to be creative within narrow guidelines. During a 14-day liver detox nutritional plan in February 2019, I started creating meals using the few select ingredients recommended for the protocol. While in the kitchen preparing food one afternoon, I had an epiphany. You know, one of those ah-ha moments when a lightbulb flickered above my head like you see in classic cartoons. I instantly realized that my creativity in the kitchen is my own personal gift, and not everyone has this ability. It was on that day *WHOLE 4 MEALS* was born!

So, my friend, I hope these recipes and meal ideas inspire you on your healthy living journey. Have some fun in the kitchen and don't be afraid to play with your food!

Be creative in Life, Love, Health, and Cooking.

Pam Terrell
Integrative Health Practitioner
Certified Hallelujah Acres Health Minister
Certified Live Food Chef

** I share my amazing journey in my book *On the Path of Love, How to Recognize Divine Guidance in Your Life*, co-authored with my husband Jeff.

Introduction to Whole Food

WHOLE 4 MEALS contains 40 recipes that utilize healthy, whole (single ingredient), and plant-centered foods with 4 ingredients plus spices. It was designed to reflect the simplicity of healthy meal preparation and to spark your personal creativity in the kitchen.

Simple is my goal, so you do not need a lot of fancy equipment to prepare food. A good blender, food processor, and vegetable spiralizer are used in recipes which are very helpful for utilizing vegetables in new ways. I also share healthy spins on a few old favorites.

You may notice I did not list breakfast, lunch, and dinner categories, but instead divided the recipes into a vegan section with meals that are served in a glass, bowl, wrap, or on a plate. Same with the animal protein section. I intentionally focused on sharing more vegan recipes because many people new to plant-centered eating are not sure where to begin when they decrease meat consumption.

What does my "normal" day of eating look like, you ask? I utilize diet variation and try to give my body a variety of foods each day, along with changing up my eating window (the hours of the day I eat food) for 1-2 days of the week. Here is a sample of what that looks like:

Monday – Friday: Standard Days

6:45am	8-16 oz of water (lemon optional)
7:00am	12 oz Cold Brew Coffee, black (recipe on page 24)
8:00am	Smoothie (includes fresh greens plus nutritional & greens powder)
12:00pm	Lunch – I choose from recipes on the following pages
5:00pm	Dinner – I choose from recipes on the following pages

You can see my "eating window" begins around 8:00am and ends around 6:00pm, which is a 10-hour window. The remaining 14 hours allow for ample digestion and healing.

Saturday: Feast Day including Flex Meal of the week

6:45am	8-16 oz of water (lemon optional)
7:00am	12 oz Cold Brew Coffee, black (recipe on page 24)
9:00am	Smoothie (includes fresh greens plus nutritional & greens powder)
2:00pm	Flex Meal (might include bread, pasta, dessert, etc. No rules for 1 meal)

Sunday: Extend the eating window and add healthy breakfast option

6:45am	8-16 oz of water (lemon optional)
7:00am	12 oz Cold Brew Coffee, black (recipe on page 24)
9:00am	Breakfast– Fancy meal with healthy pancakes, etc.
1:00pm	Lunch – I choose from recipes on the following pages
6:00pm	Dinner – I choose from recipes on the following pages

Yep, it's that easy! A couple times a month I choose to fast until dinner, drinking only 2 nutritional shakes during the day. This is what is working well for me (at this time) and I am always listening to my body, staying aware of adjustments that need to be made.

The recipes in this book are actually meals, so no need to mix and match to figure out combinations.

Each MEAL recipe contains ingredients listed in this order:
> 1 Vegan or Animal Protein
> 2 Vegetables
> 1 Fat (added after cooking)
> Spices

Why 4 ingredients? To keep it simple, for one! By using a few select food items, the digestive system does not have to work as hard. It can break down and digest food better, take a little break, then go to work on all the "stuff" that has been stored away in the fat stores of our body. It literally has time to clean house.

When we give the body what it needs, it can perform amazing tasks it was designed to do! What does it need? Nutrition. Simple as that. But that one single word has turned into the most confusing one when it comes to definitions.

So, once again, I prefer to keep it simple and stick with the foods that make sense to me to give my body. Those include healthy carbohydrates from plants: lots of vegetables, some fruit, and root vegetables.

To avoid oxidation and body inflammation, healthy fats that are not heated, but instead added *after* cooking, are ideal. Avocado, olive oil, coconut oil, raw nuts, and raw seeds are a few of the most common ones I use.

Plant protein options include: bean sprouts, beans, legumes, lentils, split mung beans, tofu (sprouted organic), hummus, chickpeas, and hemp hearts. If you choose to eat some animal protein, you might choose: anchovies, chicken, cod, Cornish hen, duck, haddock, salmon, sardines, scallops, sole, shrimp, turkey, and trout.

Please feel free to substitute any protein, vegetable, or fat with one more suitable for you. Each of our bodies is unique and we each resonate with various foods. This book is not intended to restrict tasty meals, but instead empower you to eat ample amounts of nutritious options.

Once digestion is optimized, mixing additional vegetables (more than 2) into the recipes is fine. You may also choose to use olive oil and avocado together. Whole foods such as brown rice, quinoa, oats, and additional fruits may also have a place in your diet. We are individuals and finding what works for you is the name of the game. If at any time digestion feels sluggish, coming back to these basic recipes could give your body the break it needs.

FRESH FOOD
Ideally, all foods should be as close to their whole form as possible – meaning as you would see it in nature. An example would be to predominately eat lentils vs. a lentil pasta that has been minimally processed. Hummus is fine, but please read the ingredient labels. I find the organic ones use olive oil instead of soybean, which is a better option because only organic soy products are advised. I do include a recipe for homemade hummus that is easy and equally delicious – plus you can get creative with it!

For beans you can use canned (please rinse well) or cook yourself. I do not include a recipe to prepare beans from scratch but you can follow the package instructions for the specific kind you are cooking. If you are just beginning to add these to your diet, you might want to start with ¼ cup for one meal a day. If that amount is tolerated well then increase to ½ cup and gradually work your way up to a ¾ - 1 cup serving size. We each have a different tolerance and mine seems to be around ¾ cup. Digestive enzymes might be helpful in the beginning also.

ORGANIC
To avoid putting additional toxins into our amazing bodies, organic foods are recommended, especially the ones on the Dirty Dozen list. The foods vary each year so please refer to updated information on the Dirty Dozen and Clean Fifteen on this website: https://www.ewg.org/foodnews/.

WILD PROTEIN
The meat and fish options should come from reliable sources and be free-range, organic, or wild-caught. Once again, as found in nature.

PUT A LITTLE LOVE IN IT

I personally love being in the kitchen! One integral lesson I learned from food is that it is not my enemy. Even if a food reaction occurs, I now know my body is wisely communicating with me, and I need to listen. So, as I cut, chop, spiralize, blend, and cook my body's most valuable equity – food – I energize it with love. You know, positive vibes, juju. I visualize it giving my body all it needs to repair, heal, and create balance.

GARDENING

I started to garden in 2018. On a warm sunny Florida afternoon, I was watering my raised bed garden with tears streaming down my face. My heart burst wide open releasing intense emotions. I realized my body was finally well enough to take care of something other than just myself. I was growing plants that were, in turn, growing a healthier body for me to live in! That was a very special day.

I cannot express the vibrancy my home-grown food radiates. I highly recommend it, no matter how small you choose to start.

DETOX

These *WHOLE 4 MEALS* can be used during a cleanse, detox, or on regular days. Basically, whenever you want to ease up on your digestive system. My health improved dramatically when I applied the principles from *The Rain Barrel Effect* by Dr. Stephen Cabral, including a seasonal 7-day liver detox protocol. I share that information on my website: www.PamelaTerrell.com. Perhaps you will join me!

LET'S EAT

Ok, this is a cookbook, not a textbook. My intention is to help you understand why I created this book, chose the ingredients, and how it can work for you on your health journey. Let's make some food!

Section II:

Vegan
Recipes & Meals

Seasonings & Single Recipes

The recipes listed in this section are used multiple times throughout the book in the MEALS. They are listed here for easy reference.

Taco Seasoning

1 T Chili Powder
¼ t Garlic Powder
¼ t Onion Powder
¼ t Red Pepper, crushed
¼ t Oregano
½ t Paprika
1 ½ t Cumin
1 t Sea Salt
1 t Black Pepper

1. Place all ingredients in a bowl and mix well.

2. Place in glass mason jar with lid for storage.

Homemade Hummus

1 can Chickpeas, drained
2 T Tahini
2 T Lemon Juice
1 t Cumin, ground
1 t Paprika
2 - 4 T Water
2 T Olive Oil
Garlic Powder, pinch
Sea Salt, to taste

1. Place all ingredients in food
   processor and pulse until smooth
   and creamy. Stop and scrape
   sides of container with spatula
   and add a little more water until
   desired consistency.

Cauliflower "Rice"

1 C Cauliflower, chopped
2 T Water

1. Pulse fresh chopped Cauliflower in food processor gently until a rice consistency is achieved.

2. Heat 2 T water in sauté pan on medium heat, then add riced Cauliflower. Stir frequently until slightly softened and water is absorbed, about 3-5 minutes.

Carrot Fries

1-2 C Carrots, cut into French fry shapes
Cinnamon, sprinkle
Onion Powder, sprinkle
Garlic Powder, sprinkle
Chili Powder, sprinkle

1. Preheat oven to 350 degrees.

2. On large baking sheet lined with parchment paper, spread out Carrots.

3. Sprinkle evenly with Onion Powder, Garlic Powder, Chili Powder, and Cinnamon. Adjust amounts based on your individual tastes. Use your hands to spread spices onto both sides of Carrots.

4. Bake for 45-60 minutes, until soft yet firm.

MEALS:
Glasses

Okay, so coffee isn't really a MEAL, but it is in this section since it is served in a pretty clear glass.

Cold Brew Coffee

I love the taste of coffee but it upsets my stomach. I make my own cold brew because it is less acidic, I can make it with half the caffeine, and purchase the cleanest coffee beans. It may seem like a lot of steps but it is quite easy.

1.5 oz Coffee, Organic Low Mold
    (I use Bulletproof Mentalist)
1.5 oz Coffee Decaf, Organic Low Mold
    (I use Bulletproof Decaf)
Water, cold (2-3 C)

Mason Jar 32 oz
Bamboo Filter (Organic Family)

1. Grind Coffee coarse ground.
2. Place bamboo filter into 32 oz mason jar, securing it by folding it over the edge. Put jar on scale, turn on, then add 1.5 oz of coarse ground regular coffee and 1.5 oz Decaf (3 oz total)
3. Remove from scale and pour cold Water over the coffee, filling the jar. Stir gently using a knife to make sure all grounds are moist.
4. Secure filter with the attached band. Fill with Water to top then screw on lid.
5. Place jar in refrigerator for next day. I prepare mine in the morning and let sit until the following morning (24 hours). 12 hours would work also.
6. The following day remove the filter and twist to squeeze out the remaining liquid into jar.
7. To serve, pour into glass, add ice, and dilute with water (25-50%) to taste. I know the taste is right for me when the first sip is slightly strong because it tends to dilute a little from the melting ice. Play with the ratio to find your sweet spot!

I demonstrate this recipe in a video on my YouTube channel: Pam Terrell, Author.

I Heart, Hemp Smoothie

3 T Hemp Hearts
1 C Cherries, frozen
1-2 C Leafy Greens
¼ Avocado
1 C Water
5 drops Stevia
Cinnamon, sprinkle
2-4 Basil leaves, fresh

1. Add all ingredients to blender.

2. Blend until smooth and creamy!

MEALS:

Bowls

Ah, so many beautiful foods can be served in a bowl – soups, stews, salads, and "bowls"!

Pinto Beans & "Rice"

½-1 C Pinto Beans
1 C Cauliflower Rice *(recipe page 20)*
1 C Tomato, chopped
1-2 T Olive Oil
1 T Water
Basil, fresh

1. Place cooked Cauliflower Rice in bowl.

2. Place Pinto Beans in colander and run under very hot water to rinse and heat them (or heat in small pan on stovetop), then place into bowl.

3. Add Tomato, Olive Oil, and fresh Basil.

Kidney Beans & "Rice"

½-1 C Kidney Beans
1 C Cauliflower Rice *(recipe page 20)*
½ C Onion, diced small
¼ Avocado, diced
Lime
Cilantro, fresh
Cumin, optional
Sea Salt

1. Place cooked Cauliflower Rice in bowl.

2. Place Kidney Beans in colander and run under very hot water to rinse and heat them (or heat in small pan on stovetop), then place into bowl.

3. Add Onion and Avocado then stir to mix evenly.

4. Drizzle Lime Juice on top then add Cilantro.

Tofu Taco Bowl

¼ package Tofu
1 C Cauliflower Rice *(recipe page 20)*
1 C Tomato, diced
¼ Avocado
2 T Water
1 t Taco Seasoning *(recipe page 18)*
¼ t Cumin
¼ t Sea Salt
Cilantro

1. Remove Tofu from package and use paper towels to press out water.

2. Heat 2 T Water in small skillet on medium heat and crumble Tofu with hands into pan. Add Taco Seasoning. Heat, adding more water if needed to keep from sticking.

2. Place Cauliflower in bowl, add Tofu, Tomato, Avocado, and Cilantro.

Kitchari Bowl

½ C Split Yellow Mung Beans (Dahl)
1 C Cauliflower Rice *(recipe page 20)*
1 C Kale, chopped fine no stems
1-2 T Coconut Oil
½ C Water + 1 C for soaking
1 t Cumin
½ t Fennel
½ t Mustard
½ t Coriander
½ t Ginger, grated
¼ t Turmeric
¼ t Sea Salt
Cilantro
¼ Lime

1. Soak Split Yellow Mung Beans in 1 C Water for at least 30 minutes.

2. Rinse, drain, and add to medium saucepan along with ½ C Water and Kale. Cover and cook until kale and Mung Beans are soft, about 15-20 minutes.

3. Add Cauliflower, Cumin, Fennel, Mustard, Coriander, Ginger, Turmeric, and Sea Salt. Stir, cover, and cook 5-10 minutes until Cauliflower is soft but firm.

4. Place in bowl, stir in Coconut Oil, then top with fresh Cilantro and a squeeze of Lime.

Buddha Bowl

½-1 C Black Beans
1 C Cauliflower Rice *(recipe page 20)*
1 C Kale, chopped, stems removed
¼ Avocado, sliced
2 T Water + 2 T
Garlic Powder, dash
Sea Salt, to taste
Black Pepper, optional

1. Heat 2 T Water in skillet on medium heat, add Kale and Garlic Powder. Cover, stirring occasionally until wilted.

2. Place Black Beans in colander and run under very hot water to rinse and heat them (or heat in small pan on stovetop).

3. In medium bowl place Cauliflower Rice, Black Beans beside it, then Kale, and lastly Avocado to create a lovely bowl visually. Add Salt & Pepper if needed.

Buddha Bowl with Sweet Potato

½-1 C Black Beans
1 C Sweet Potato, sliced rounds
1 C Kale, chopped, stems removed
¼ Avocado, diced
½ C Water + 2 T
Garlic Powder, dash
Sea Salt, to taste
Black Pepper, optional

1. Steam Sweet Potato in sauce pan with ½ C Water until soft.

2. Heat 2 T Water in skillet on medium heat, add Kale and Garlic Powder then stir occasionally until wilted.

3. Place Black Beans in colander and run under very hot water to rinse and heat them (or heat in small pan on stovetop).

4. In medium bowl place Sweet Potato, Black Beans beside it, then Kale, and lastly Avocado to create a lovely bowl visually. Add Salt & Pepper if needed.

Chili – serves 2

1 Can, 15 oz, Kidney Beans
1 Can, 14 oz. Tomatoes
1 C Onions, chopped
½ Avocado
2 T Water
1 t Garlic Powder
1 t Chili Powder
½ t Oregano
Chipotle Chili Powder, *pinch if you like spicy chili*
Sea Salt, to taste
Cilantro, fresh (optional)

1. Heat Water and Onions in medium saucepan on medium heat. Stir frequently and cook until Onions are soft and clear. Add a bit more water if they start to stick on pan.

2. Add Kidney Beans, Tomatoes with juice, Chili Powder, Oregano, and Chipotle Chili Powder. Stir occasionally until heated, at least 5-10 minutes.

3. Place Chili in bowl, top with Avocado, and sprinkle with fresh Cilantro. Add Sea Salt to taste.

Chili "Rice" Bowl

1 C Pinto Beans
1 C Tomatoes, diced
1 C Cauliflower Rice *(recipe page 20)*
¼ Avocado, diced
1 t Dried Onion Flakes
½ t Onion Powder
½ t Garlic Powder
½ - 1 t Chili Powder
¼ t Oregano
Sea Salt

1. Heat Pinto Beans, Tomatoes, Onion Powder, Garlic Powder, Chili Powder, and Oregano in medium saucepan on medium heat. Stir occasionally until heated, about 5 minutes. Cook longer for flavors to meld, up to 30 minutes.

2. Place Chili in bowl, Cauliflower beside it, Avocado on top, and sprinkle with Cilantro. Add Sea Salt to taste.

White Chili

1 C Navy Beans
1 C Mushrooms, chopped
1 C Onions, diced
1-2 T Coconut Oil, unflavored
½ C Vegetable Broth
1 t Italian Seasoning
Rosemary, pinch
¼ t Sea Salt
Black Pepper, pinch

1. Heat Vegetable Broth in medium
   saucepan on medium heat. Add
   Mushrooms and Onions and
   cook until softened. Mushrooms
   will begin to turn slightly brown.

2. Add Navy Beans, Italian
   Seasoning, Rosemary, Sea Salt,
   and Black Pepper to pan. Cover
   and cook until heated, stirring
   occasionally, about 10 minutes.

3. Stir in Coconut Oil then Scoop
   into bowl.

Lentil Cabbage Soup

½-1 C Lentils, cooked
1 C Cabbage, shredded
1 C Rainbow Carrots, chopped
1-2 T Olive Oil
½ C Water
1 t Minced Dried Onion
1-2 t Tomato Paste
½ t Italian Seasoning
¼ t Onion Powder
¼ t Garlic Powder
¼ t Parsley
1 C Vegetable Broth
¼ t Sea Salt, to taste

1. Sauté Carrots and Water in medium saucepan on medium heat until soft, 5-10 minutes.

2. Add Cabbage, Lentils, Dried Onion, Tomato Paste, Garlic Powder, Parsley, Italian Seasoning, Onion Powder, and Vegetable Broth. Stir to mix well. Simmer for 15 minutes.

3. Place in bowl then stir in Olive Oil. Add Sea Salt to taste.

Hearty Broccoli Soup

½ C Lentils, cooked
2 C Broccoli
2 T Olive Oil
¼ t Onion Powder
¼ t Parsley
¼ C Vegetable Broth
Water, to steam Broccoli
Tomato, garnish optional

1. Cook Lentils per package instructions.

2. Steam Broccoli in Water.

3. Add Lentils, Broccoli, Olive Oil, Onion Powder, Parsley, and Vegetable Broth to Vitamix or Blender. Puree until smooth and creamy.

Creamy Asparagus Soup – serves 4

2 C Green Lentils, cooked
2 lbs. Asparagus, ends trimmed
2 C Onion, diced
¼ C Water
2-4 T Olive Oil
3 ½ C Vegetable Broth
2 cloves Garlic, minced
1 ½ t Sea Salt
¼ t Black Pepper
1 t Rosemary fresh (or ½ t dry)
1 t Thyme, fresh (or ½ t dry)
1 T Lemon Juice

1. Cook Lentils according to package directions (1 ½ C dry to cook up to 2 C).

2. Cut Asparagus into 2" pieces.

3. In large pot add Water and Onions. Cook over medium heat, stirring occasionally for 3-5 minutes until Onion is translucent.

4. Add Garlic, Sea Salt, and Pepper then sauté for 2 minutes.

5. Add Asparagus and continue cooking over medium heat for 5 minutes.

6. Reduce heat to medium-low. Add Rosemary, Thyme, and Vegetable Broth. Cover and simmer for 7-10 minutes, or until Asparagus is tender.

7. Place Asparagus mixture, Lentils, and Olive Oil into blender and blend until smooth and creamy.

MEALS:

"Pasta"

"Pasta" can be made using so many vegetables, all you need is a kitchen appliance that spiralizes. Yes, food can be fun!

Sweet Potato Spirals & Beans

½ – 1 C White Beans
1 C Pasta Sauce
1 C Sweet Potato, spiralized
1-2 T Olive Oil
¼ t Italian Seasoning
Sea Salt, sprinkle
Basil, fresh

1. Preheat oven to 425 degrees.

2. Peel then Spiralize Sweet Potato. Place on cookie sheet lined with parchment paper and sprinkle Sea Salt.

3. Bake Sweet Potato spirals for 10 minutes, until tender.

4. Place Beans in bowl, add Olive Oil, Italian Seasoning, and pinch of Sea Salt. Stir then let marinate.

5. Heat Pasta Sauce in small pan on stovetop.

6. Place Sweet Potato on plate, top with Pasta Sauce, Bean mixture, and fresh Basil.

MEALS:
Wraps

Wraps have a whole new meaning when eating a plant-centered whole food diet! Greens are sturdy and bring a vibrant twist to a meal.

Collard Hummus Wrap

½-1 C Hummus
1-2 Large Collard Leaves
1 C Red Peppers, diced
½-1 C Sprouts
¼ Avocado

1. Spread out Collard Leaves on counter.   Cut out the stem about half way up leaf to remove because they are too fibrous to eat.

2. Spread Hummus on one side of each.

3. Sprinkle Red Peppers, Sprouts, and Avocado on same side.

4. Roll and slice!

Nori Hummus Wrap

½ C Hummus
1-2 Nori Sheets, raw
½-1 C Carrots, shredded
¼ Avocado
Sprouts, sprinkle

1. Spread out Nori Sheets on large cutting board.

2. Spread Hummus on one side of each, covering about half of the sheet.

3. Sprinkle Carrots, Sprouts, and Avocado on same side.

4. Roll as tightly as possible. Wet the final edge of the wrap with a little water then finish rolling. The moistness on the sheet will help it hold together.

5. Slice with a very sharp knife!

Taco Leaf

½-1 C Pinto Beans
1-2 Large Romaine Leaves
1 C Tomatoes, diced
¼ Avocado
¼ - ½ t Cumin
1-2 t Water
Sea Salt, pinch
Cilantro

1. Smash Pinto Beans in bowl with fork. Add Cumin, Water, and Sea Salt, using only enough Water to hold beans together.

2. Place Bean mixture on Romaine Leaf. Add Tomatoes, Avocado, and Cilantro.

Tofu Taco

½-1 C Tofu
1-2 Large Romaine Leaves
1 C Tomatoes, diced
¼ Avocado
2 T Water
Taco Seasoning *(recipe page 18)*
Cumin
Cilantro
Sea Salt

1. Place Water in sauté pan on medium heat. Add Tofu, crumbling with hands while adding to skillet.

2. Add Taco Seasoning and Cumin, stirring to prevent sticking, until warm.

3. On large Romaine Leaves place Tofu, Tomatoes, Avocado, and Cilantro. Sprinkle with Sea Salt.

Fajita Leaf

½-1 C Tofu
1-2 Large Romaine Leaves
1 C Red Peppers, diced
¼ Avocado
2 -4 T Water
Taco Seasoning *(recipe page 18)*
Cumin
Cilantro
Sea Salt
Lime Juice *(optional)*

1. Place 2 T Water in sauté pan on medium heat. Add Red Peppers, stirring frequently, until softened.

2. In a separate skillet on medium heat, add 2 T Water and Tofu, crumbling with hands while adding to skillet. Sprinkle Taco Seasoning and Cumin, stirring to prevent sticking, until warm.

3. On large Romaine Leaves place Tofu, Red Peppers, and Avocado. Sprinkle with Sea Salt and a squeeze of Lime Juice if desired.

MEALS:

Plates

I keep an assortment of plates in my kitchen to add an additional layer of beauty and interest to a simple meal.

Beans & Greens

½ - 1 C Navy Beans
1 C Kale, chopped
1 C Brussel Sprouts, sliced in half
1-2 T Olive Oil
¼ C Water + 2 T
Garlic Powder
Sea Salt
Black Pepper

1. Heat ¼ C Water in large pan on medium heat. Add Brussel Sprouts, cover, and steam until soft, stirring occasionally. If they start to stick to pan then add a tiny bit more water until vegetables are tender.

2. In a separate pan on medium heat, add 2 T Water, Kale, and pinch of Garlic Powder. Cover and simmer until soft, at least 5 minutes.

3. Place Navy Beans in colander and run under very hot water to rinse and heat them (or heat in small pan on stovetop).

4. Place on plate of choice then drizzle Olive Oil on top. Season with Salt and Pepper as desired.

Beans & Sprouts

½ - 1 C Navy Beans
1 C Onions, large thin slices
1 C Brussel Sprouts, sliced in half
¼ Avocado, sliced
¼ C Water
Sea Salt
Black Pepper

1. Heat ¼ C Water in large pan on medium heat. Add Brussel Sprouts then Onions on top. Cover and steam until soft, stirring occasionally. If they start to stick to the pan then add a tiny bit more water until vegetables are tender.

2. Place Navy Beans in colander and run under very hot water to rinse and heat them (or heat in small pan on stovetop).

3. Place on plate of choice and season with Salt and Pepper as desired.

Beans, Greens & Chard

½ - 1 C Navy Beans
1 C Swiss Chard, chopped
1 C Green Beans
1-2 T Olive Oil
¼ C + 2 T Vegetable Broth
Garlic Powder, pinch
Sea Salt
Black Pepper

1. Heat ¼ C Vegetable Broth in large pan on medium heat and add Green Beans. Cover and steam until soft, stirring occasionally.

2. In a separate pan, add 2 T Vegetable Broth on medium heat then add chopped Swiss Chard and Garlic Powder. Cover and simmer until soft, about 3 minutes.

3. Place Navy Beans in colander and run under very hot water to rinse and heat them (or heat in small pan on stovetop).

4. Place all on plate and drizzle with Olive Oil.

Spicy Tofu

1 C Tofu, sliced ¼ " thick
1 C Cauliflower
1 C Brussel Sprouts
1-2 T Olive Oil
½ C Water + ½ C + 2 T
¼ t Paprika
½ t Garlic Powder
¼ t Fennel
¼ t Sea Salt
Black Pepper, pinch
Cayenne, pinch

1. Heat ½ C Water in small pan on medium-high heat. Add Brussel Sprouts, cover, and steam until soft about 8-10 minutes.

2. Heat ½ C Water in sauce pan on medium-high heat. Add Cauliflower and steam until soft 5-10 minutes. When done, drain then place in blender with a pinch of Sea Salt and 1 T Olive Oil. Blend until smooth. Keep in blender covered to keep warm.

3. Mix Paprika, Garlic Powder, Fennel, Sea Salt, Black Pepper, and Cayenne in small mixing bowl.

4. Heat sauté pan on medium heat, add 2 T Water and slices of Tofu. Sprinkle spice mix evenly on one side, then turn Tofu over and dust other side. Turn to prevent sticking, until hot.

5. Place on plate then drizzle with 1 T Olive Oil. Salt and Pepper to taste.

Hummus Delight

½ - 1 C Hummus
1 C Brussel Sprouts, sliced in half
1 C Onions, large sliced
1-2 T Olive Oil
¼ C Water
Sea Salt
Black Pepper
Garlic Powder (optional)

1. Heat ¼ C Water in large pan on medium heat and add Brussel Sprouts first then Onions on top. Cover and steam until soft, about 10-12 minutes, stirring occasionally. If they start to stick to pan then add a tiny bit more water. Vegetables should be soft yet firm.

2. Place on plate, scoop Hummus in the middle, drizzle with Olive Oil, then add Salt and Pepper if desired.

Hummus Rounds

½ - 1 C Hummus
1 C Cucumber, sliced
1 C Carrots, diced
¼ Avocado

1. Spread out sliced Cucumbers on plate,

2. Spoon Hummus on each round.

3. Top with Carrots and Avocado pieces.

Section III:

Turkey, Chicken & Fish Meals

If your diet contains animal protein, I have included some turkey, chicken, and fish ideas.

MEALS:
Bowls

I have included one recipe in this section, but any of the Vegan Bowls can be used here by substituting with an animal protein.

Turkey Chili – serves 2

8 oz Turkey, ground
16-20 oz can Tomatoes, diced
1 ¾ C Onions, diced
½ Avocado
2 t Garlic Powder
2 t Chili Powder
½ t Oregano
½ t Sea Salt
¼ t Chipotle Chili Powder
Cilantro

1. Brown Turkey and Onions together in medium-large skillet on medium heat. Break up meat with spatula as it cooks, about 10 minutes.

2. Stir in Tomatoes, Garlic Powder, Chili Powder, Oregano, Sea Salt, and Chipotle Powder. Mix well, cover, and simmer on low, stirring occasionally.

3. Cook at least 20-30 minutes, allowing spices to meld together.

4. Serve in a bowl with diced Avocado and fresh Cilantro on top.

MEALS:

"Pasta"

Give traditional meals a healthy spin and spiralize some veggies. Beautiful and delicious!

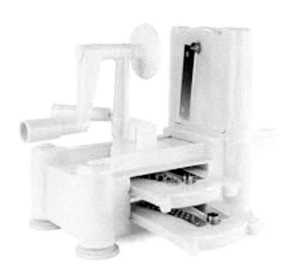

Chicken "Pasta"

4 oz Chicken Breast tenders
1-2 C Zucchini, spiraled
1 C Pasta Sauce
1-2 T Olive Oil
Italian Seasoning
Garlic
Sea Salt
Basil, fresh

1. Preheat oven to 375 degrees.
2. Sprinkle Italian Seasoning and Garlic Powder on both sides of Chicken. Place on parchment lined cookie sheet, place in oven, and cook for 15-20 minutes.
3. While Chicken is in the oven, place spiralized Zucchini in bowl with a pinch of Sea Salt. Using your hands, distribute the salt and gently squeeze the "pasta". This will release some of the water to prevent from getting mushy during cooking. Let sit 5 min then squeeze and drain as much water as possible.
4. Heat Pasta Sauce in small saucepan.
5. Add Zucchini "pasta" to another skillet on medium heat and stir frequently to prevent sticking. Heat a few minutes until Zucchini is hot.
6. Plate "Pasta" and Chicken with Pasta Sauce on top, drizzle with Olive Oil, and add fresh Basil.

Turkey Meatball "Pasta" – serves 2

8 oz Turkey, ground
4 oz Zucchini, shredded
16 oz Zucchini, spiralized
2-3 C Pasta sauce
2-4 T Olive Oil
½ t Onion Powder
½ t Garlic Powder
1 t Italian Seasoning
¼ t Sage
¼ t Oregano
¼ t Basil
¼ t Sea Salt
Black Pepper, pinch
Basil, fresh

1. Preheat oven to 350 degrees. Line baking sheet with parchment paper.
2. In large mixing bowl, combine Turkey, shredded Zucchini, Onion Powder, Garlic Powder, Italian Seasoning, Sage, Oregano, Basil, Sea Salt, and Black Pepper. Mix with fork until evenly combined. Mixture will be moist. Using small ice cream scoop, scoop mixture and place on baking sheet. Repeat making small meatballs. Place in oven and cook for 15 minutes or until Turkey reaches 175 degrees.
3. While in oven, place spiralized Zucchini in bowl with a pinch of Sea Salt. Using your hands, distribute the salt and gently squeeze the "pasta". This will release some of the water to prevent from getting mushy during cooking. Let sit 5 min then squeeze and drain as much water as possible.
4. Heat Pasta Sauce in small sauce pan.
5. Add Zucchini "pasta" to another skillet on medium heat and stir frequently to prevent sticking. Heat a few minutes until Zucchini is hot.
6. Plate Zucchini "pasta", mini meatballs, and Pasta Sauce then drizzle with Olive Oil and top with fresh Basil.

MEALS:

Wraps

Green leaves elevate whole food to a new level! Collards, romaine, and soft leafy lettuce are refreshing elements complimenting many dishes.

Fish Taco

4 oz Cod
2 Romaine Leaves
1 C Tomato, diced
¼ Avocado, diced
Taco Seasoning *(recipe page 18)*
Cumin
Sea Salt
Cilantro, optional

1. Heat small skillet on medium heat. Place Cod in pan and sprinkle with Taco Seasoning. Cover and cook for 5 minutes. Turn fish over. Cook until flakey.

2. Once cooked, place fish in bowl and flake with a fork. Add Cumin or Sea Salt to taste.

3. Place large Romaine Leaves on plate. Distribute Cod, Tomatoes, and Avocado. Garnish with Cilantro, if desired.

T.L.T. (Turkey, Lettuce, Tomato)

4 oz Turkey Breast, sliced
2-3 Romaine Leaves
1 C Tomato, sliced
¼ Avocado, sliced thin
Sea Salt
Black Pepper

1. Place Romaine Leaves on plate.
Top with sliced Turkey Breast,
Tomatoes, and Avocado.

2. Sprinkle with Salt and Pepper.

MEALS:

Plates

It's easy to turn traditional meals into healthy whole food fuel for your body!

Thanksgiving Basic

4 oz Turkey Breast, Roasted
1 C Cauliflower
1 C Green Beans
1-2 T Olive Oil
½ C Water + ¼ C
Onion Powder
Garlic Powder
Sea Salt
Black Pepper

1. Place Green Beans in medium skillet with ¼ C Water, Onion Powder, and Garlic Powder. Cover and steam, stirring occasionally until tender, about 10-15 minutes.

2. Heat ½ C Water in sauce pan on medium-high heat. Add Cauliflower and steam until soft 5-10 minutes. When done, drain then place in blender with a pinch of Sea Salt and 1 T Olive Oil. Blend until smooth. Keep in blender covered to keep warm.

3. When Green Beans are almost done, Slice Turkey and place in skillet on top of Green Beans to gently warm.

4. Plate pureed Cauliflower, Green Beans, and Turkey. Drizzle with Olive Oil and season with Salt and Pepper.

Thanksgiving, Take 2

4 oz Turkey breast
1 C Cauliflower
1 Sweet Potato, small
1-2 T Olive Oil
2 T Water
Salt
Black Pepper

1. Preheat oven to 425°.
Poke small-medium sized sweet
potatoes several times with a fork
then place on parchment lined
baking sheet. Bake until tender, 45
to 60 minutes.

2. Heat ½ C Water in sauce pan on
medium-high heat. Add Cauliflower
and steam until soft 5-10 minutes.
When done, drain then place in
blender with a pinch of Sea Salt
and 1 T Olive Oil. Blend until
smooth. Keep in blender covered
to keep warm.

3. In small skillet heat Turkey in
small amount of water to gently
steam it warm.

4. Plate pureed Cauliflower, Sweet
Potato, and Turkey. Drizzle with
Olive Oil and season with Salt and Pepper.

Turkey Meatloaf – serves 2

8 oz Turkey, ground
2 C Cauliflower
2 C Green Beans, steamed
2-4 T Olive Oil
½ C Water + ¼ C

<u>Spices for Meatloaf</u>
½ t Onion Powder
½ t Garlic Powder
½ t Italian Seasoning
¼ t Sage
¼ t Oregano
¼ t Basil
¼ t Sea Salt
Black Pepper, pinch

<u>Spices for Green Beans</u>
½ t Onion Powder
½ t Garlic Powder

1. Preheat oven to 350 degrees.
2. Line baking sheet with parchment paper.
3. In large mixing bowl, combine Turkey, Onion Powder, Garlic Powder, Italian Seasoning, Sage, Oregano, Basil, Sea Salt, and Black Pepper. Mix with fork until evenly combined.
4. Using medium ice cream scoop, scoop mixture and place on lined baking sheet.
5. Place in oven and cook for 20 minutes or until Turkey reaches 175 degrees.
6. Heat ½ C Water in sauce pan on medium-high heat. Add Cauliflower and steam until soft 5-10 minutes. When done, drain then place in blender with a pinch of Sea Salt and 1 T Olive Oil. Blend until smooth. Keep in blender covered to keep warm.
7. Place Green Beans in medium skillet with ¼ C Water, Onion Powder, and Garlic Powder. Cover and steam, stirring occasionally until tender, about 10-15 minutes.
9. Plate pureed Cauliflower, Green Beans, and Meatloaf. Drizzle with Olive Oil and season with Salt and Pepper.

Chicken Poppers & Carrot Fries

(makes 3-4 servings Poppers)
1 lb. Chicken, ground
16 oz Zucchini
Carrot Fries *(recipe page 21)*
¼ Avocado, sliced
2 t Onion Powder
1 t Cumin
1 t Parsley
1 t Garlic
1 t Sea Salt
Black Pepper, pinch

1. Heat oven to 400 degrees.

2. Grate Zucchini in food processor, no need to peel.

3. In large mixing bowl, add Chicken, Zucchini, Onion Powder, Cumin, Parsley, Garlic, Sea Salt, and Black Pepper. Mix with large spoon until combined and moist.

4. Line large baking sheet with parchment paper. Using medium sized ice cream scoop, scoop mixture into rounds and place on cookie sheet leaving a little space between. Bake for 20-25 minutes.

5. Bake Carrot Fries per recipe.

6. Plate Chicken, Carrot Fries, and sliced Avocado. Season with Salt and Pepper, as desired.

Legs & Fries

2 Chicken Legs
Carrot Fries *(recipe page 21)*
1 C Kale, chopped
½ Avocado
Onion Powder
Garlic Powder
Paprika
Sea Salt
Black Pepper

Kale
Vegetable Broth
Garlic Powder
Cayenne, slight pinch
3 Stevia drops

Avocado Dip
½ t Cinnamon
4 drops Stevia

1. Preheat oven to 350 degrees.
2. Bake Carrot Fries per recipe.
3. Dust Chicken with Onion Powder, Garlic Powder, Paprika, Sea Salt, and Pepper.
4. Bake chicken on parchment paper lined cookie sheet for 30-40 min until meat thermometer reads 175 degrees.
5. Remove Kale from stem and finely chop. In medium pan add Vegetable Broth, Kale, Garlic Powder, a small pinch of Cayenne, and 3 drops of Stevia. Cook on medium heat until soft and wilted, about 15 minutes.
7. While all is cooking, make Avocado Dip. Mash Avocado, Cinnamon, and Stevia with a fork until creamy smooth.
8. Plate Chicken Legs and Carrot Fries on plate. Use a ramekin for Avocado Dip and a small bowl for Kale to retain juice.

Baked Salmon

4-6 oz Wild Sockeye Salmon
1 C Asparagus spears, ends trimmed
1 C Broccoli
1-2 T Olive Oil
½ C Water + ¼ C
Lemon slices
Thyme
Sea Salt

1. Preheat oven to 400 degrees.

2. Dry Salmon with paper towel.
Place in parchment paper lined
glass baking dish. Sprinkle Thyme,
Sea Salt, and place a couple
Lemon slices on top. Bake Salmon
for 12-15 minutes.

3. Heat ½ C Water in sauce pan on
medium-high heat. Add Broccoli
and steam until soft 5-10 minutes.
When done, drain then place in
blender with a pinch of Sea Salt
and 1 T Olive Oil. Blend until
smooth. Keep in blender covered
to keep warm.

4. Place Asparagus in medium pan
with ¼ C Water over medium-high heat. Cover and steam until tender, about 10
minutes.

5. Place Salmon, Broccoli puree, and Asparagus on plate and drizzle with Olive Oil,
Salt, and Pepper.

Made in the
USA
Monee, IL